Transform Your Money Mindset
"Simple Steps for Financial Fitness"

By
Audrey D. Washington

"Transform Your Money Mindset –
Simple Steps for Financial Fitness"

Publisher contact information:
Audrey D. Washington
Fiercely Financial Coaching
547 North Avenue, Suite 169
New Rochelle, NY 10801
www.fiercelyfinancial.com

Ordering Information:
https://www.createspace.com/6324562
Printed in the United States of America
ISBN 978-0-692733554

Fiercely Financial Coaching
www.fiercelyfinancial.com

In memory of:

My Dad
George W. Washington

My Great-Grandmother
Grace Sumpter ("Nana")

My Grandparents
Charles B. Washington, Sr. and
Mary Edmonds Washington

My Sister-Friend
Dr. Bridgette S. Cheeks

Thank you:

To Derrick for your love, support,
encouragement and for keeping me laughing.

To my Sheroes:
Mommy - Rev. Girdie B. Washington
Grandma – Blanche Sumpter

To Kelly, Kirby, Seth, Nolan and Zalen.

To my aunts, my uncles, my cousins, in-laws –
Blakemores, Briggs, Buggs, Edmonds, Franks,
Hills, Kings, McGhees, Peermans, Reids,
Sumpters and Washingtons.

Thank you to my many friends.
If I start to name each of you,
I know I will miss someone.
So I will just say "love and thanks" to you all!

Thank you to my Auntie – Ethel L. Sumpter
for editing the book.

Thanks and Appreciation to my Readers
for your time and feedback:
Candace, Cynthia, Gail, Girdie, Jill, Jordan,
Kelly, Kirby, Lauren, Pauline, Rodney,
Seth, Stacie, Stan and Stephanie.

Table of Contents

Pages

Introduction

I decided to write *"Transform Your Money Mindset"* because in my many years of financial coaching, I have seen people struggle to achieve their financial goals. I should add that most often the struggle was not because of lack of money. I began my financial coaching career working with clients who wanted to purchase their first home. One of the things that I noticed was that not everyone who received coaching or took a homebuyer course purchased a home. Of course, clients had various reasons for why they did not move forward but I was more struck by the people who had been trying to purchase for over 5 years.

Home buying for most people is a long-term goal but the clients I am talking about had not made any progress over the 5 years. They were still in the same place in terms of saving for their down payment or rebuilding their credit that they were when they first started.

I began to listen more closely to the reasons my clients gave for not moving forward. As I began to talk to my clients and listen to why they were not achieving their goal of homeownership, I noticed there were similar issues that were hindering their success. I also realized that the approach to working with clients was to give them the technical skills they needed to move through the home buying process. However, because there was no information given to them about the importance of shifting their Money Mindset it made it difficult for them to be successful.

It is similar to athletes. The most exceptional athletes train hard to perfect their athletic skills but they also work hard to develop their mindset. Mindset is what usually separates those with great athletic abilities from those with exceptional athletic careers. It is the work on their mindset that pushes them to train harder. It is the work on their mindset that pushes them forward when their bodies want to give up. It is the work on their mindset that helps them realize the success they are seeking.

It is the same for your financial goals and your Money Mindset. You set your financial goals using the technical skills and knowledge that you have. However, it is your Money Mindset that will keep you focused and move you forward to achieve your financial goals. Just having the technical skills is not enough. You have to *"Transform Your Money Mindset"*. Even if you know what to do, your Money Mindset will determine if you will achieve it or not.

As you read *"Transform Your Money Mindset"* take the time to complete the exercises at the end of each chapter. Doing the exercises is an important part of the process. Keep a notebook or journal with you and write down the thoughts that come to mind as you are reading the book. Highlight the sentences that resonate with you and write down how they made you feel.

"Transform Your Money Mindset" is designed to meet you where you are in your money and finance journey. This book is for you if you are just starting out in the work world, have been working for some years and even for those of you at or close to retirement. Take your time reading and your Money Mindset will be transformed!

Chapter One
Your Childhood Money Story

All of our life experiences, both good and not so good, shape who we are. Of course it's easy to see how the good experiences helped to support our growth and development in a positive way. The not so good experiences can have both a positive or negative impact on us. Our childhood years are sometimes referred to as our "formative years" meaning this is the time that we are formed and molded into who we will become as adults. This involves all parts of us – mentally, spiritually, emotionally and physically. As we grow up, we develop many stories including our *Childhood Money Story* that stay with us and sometimes become our story forever until we say "I want a new story!"

I will share my own *Childhood Money Story*. I was an Army brat that lived with both of my parents. Our family travelled for the first few years of my life starting with my birth in Germany and then onto New Jersey, Japan, North Carolina and Connecticut. When I was 7 years old we moved back to New Jersey and so the Jersey Shore is home for me. My Dad was career military and worked full-time on Army bases but he always had several side jobs including bartending and using his pick-up truck to move people and do other odd jobs. After he retired from the Army, he worked full-time and also owned two shoe repair businesses (my grandfather also owned a shoe repair business). We lived in our own home in a middle class neighborhood. My mom stayed at home in the early years of my life but by the time I was in middle school she went to college and began working outside of the home. Both of my parents were college graduates.

We always had food in the house. The lights were never turned off. We always had clothes, shoes and gifts at Christmas. We had 2 cars and when my sister, brother and I were able to drive, Daddy always purchased a 3rd car for us to drive. Mommy wanted us to learn how to play the piano so my parents brought a piano and we took piano lessons although kicking and screaming because we didn't like it. (One of my major regrets is that I didn't stick with that!)

I recall that we took a vacation to visit family in Georgia and we went to Six Flags which was a fun trip! Our regular visits to family in Connecticut, South Carolina, Virginia and Washington, DC were like mini vacations. My mom would take us to New York City to explore, we always went to Radio City for the holiday show and my Dad took us to the beach in Sandy Hook often. I saw in my parents how giving they were to others. When we would travel to see relatives, my parents always gave money to the older relatives and children.

While we had all of these things and I saw my parents' giving spirit, somehow I felt like we didn't have a lot of money. I felt like money was scarce. So, I rarely if ever asked for anything. I especially did not ask for anything unless it was a need. I used to watch ice skating on television and I just loved how they would glide around the rink. I wanted to learn how to ice skate badly. It is still one of those sentences I start with "I wish I had..." but I had a conversation in my own head that said this is expensive and Mommy and Daddy cannot afford that so "don't ask".

I think about this from time to time and try to remember a particular incident or conversation that made me think that we only had enough money for the basics – food, clothing, shelter and that we did not have money for things that we wanted. Even though all the things that I can recall showed that there was abundance in our life. We had all we needed and much of what we wanted. We did fun things and there was never a time when we went without. Yet I still felt like there was lack in having the things we wanted.

I know how my *Childhood Money Story* has shaped my financial life and actions. I saw my parents giving as a good thing and so I gave too. Too often I gave when I really did not have it to give, which put me into financial hardship and made me feel anger and resentment towards the persons I helped and even more so towards myself. I am still a giver financially but I do not do so when it will cause me a financial hardship. I also focus more on giving of my time and talent. My thinking has also shifted as it pertains to having things that I want. I understand there is nothing wrong with having some of the things I want as long as there is balance.

We each have our own *Childhood Money Story* and it shapes the way we think about money, manage money and make money. Knowing your *Childhood Money Story* is the start of the process to *Transform Your Money Mindset*. It might be painful to go backwards but the insight you gain will be invaluable and I believe will help you to move forward. Sharing your *Childhood Money Story* with your siblings, parents and close relatives may encourage them to share their Story and may give you some answers to yours.

Money Mindset Transformation Exercise Chapter 1: <u>Your Childhood Money Story</u>. (Allow at least 1 hour. You will need pen and paper. You will need to go deep within yourself. Choose a time when you won't be interrupted and you don't need to go anywhere after.)

Sit in a quiet place where you are not distracted. Take some quiet time to think about your own *Childhood Money Story*. Review the questions below, then close your eyes and take 5 – 10 deep breaths. Read the questions again and let your thoughts flow. Write down everything that comes to mind, even if it seems not related.

Once you answer these questions, think about how your *Childhood Money Story* has shaped the way you manage your money and finances.

1. What did you feel about money as a child?
2. What did you observe about money in your home?
3. What things did your parents, grandparents or other relatives say to you about money?
4. What discussions did you hear about money in your home?
5. Did you feel that money was lacking?
6. Did you feel that money was in abundance?
7. Did you have the things that you needed?
8. Did you feel that you could ask for the things that you wanted?
9. Did you get the things that you asked for?
10. What was one item that you truly wanted or the one thing that you truly wanted to do growing up? Did you get it or get to do it and how did that make you feel? If not, how did that make you feel?

Once you answer these questions, think about how your *Childhood Money Story* has shaped the way you manage your money and finances. Take 5 – 10 deep breaths and answer these questions:

1. How has my *Childhood Money Story* made me handle my money and finances?
2. What changes do I need to make?
3. Why do I need to make these changes?
4. When I make these changes what will be my desired outcome?
5. What tools and resources do I need to make these changes?

Chapter Two
Nana
"If you make a dollar, save a dime."

Saving is the foundation of financial fitness. Understanding the importance of "rainy day" savings and retirement savings will help put you on the path to Financial Fitness. Our focus in this chapter will be on "rainy day" savings but for your overall financial planning you should include a plan for your retirement savings. When we hear the term "saving for a rainy day" we know it's not really about rain but it is about saving for an emergency situation.

I tried to think how this saying related to rain. I believe that it is a very old saying perhaps from a time when people did manual labor outside. So the idea is that if it rained, you did not work, if you did not work, you did not get paid. Thus, the rainy day savings.

My concept of saving came at a very young age from my great-grandmother on my Mom's side. My great-grandmother, Grace Sumpter whom we called "Nana" was born in 1904 on St. Helena Island, South Carolina. Nana went to school briefly but sometime around age 7 or 8 she got sick with a high fever and while she survived what we believe was rheumatic fever it caused her right foot to turn in and upside down. After that Nana never went back to school and as a result she could write her name but she could not read or write. Although Nana did not have hardly any formal education, she was wise, smart and most of all very loving.

Nana worked on a vegetable farm and in a seafood factory in South Carolina. When she moved to Stamford, Connecticut she worked as a domestic caring for other people's children and cleaning their homes. And in her later years, she had a few children that she would care for in her home.

Nana never made a lot of money but family members knew that if they needed a couple of dollars that Nana would have it. While Nana or Mama Grace as many in the family and community called her, was physically disabled and could not read or write, she had a saying "If you make a dollar, save a dime."

We know that saving is the foundation for any good financial plan. But what did Nana know about financial planning? How did Nana come to understand that we had to save? That we could not spend all that we made? Even with her limited education, Nana knew the importance of saving.

When I think about Nana, I wonder about her Childhood Money Story. I know that she did not have a good childhood. I know that her disability limited her earning potential. Nana's simple quote "If you make a dollar, save a dime" means that she understood the value of saving for a rainy day. Putting something aside for later when things might be tight or when you wanted to do something or buy something.

In living by this principle, Nana had a bigger dream in mind. Nana knew that if she saved a dime from each dollar she earned that she would be able to serve her family in a bigger way. Although Nana did not earn a lot of money, her savings principle created a foundation for financial stability for herself and her family. When there was a financial need in the family, Nana could assist. Nana could serve her family.

The key to financial fitness and transformation is to commit to regular savings. Saving 10% of every dollar you make is a good goal. But if you feel like you can't do that, then consider saving 5% and then work up to 10%. If you are not saving anything, start small saving $10 a month which is $120 a year. Most people think "$10 a month is nothing" but if you are not saving anything isn't $120 better than zero? Of course!

A little trick with saving is that it is more about the habit than the amount. When you commit to saving $10 a month, are consistent and do not touch it, over time it will get easier to save larger amounts of money. Most people think "If I can't save $100 from each paycheck it's not worth it" but a little is always better than nothing.

Think about layaway. Layaway worked because it was easier for people to go to the store and put $10 or $20 dollars on the item over a period of time until it was paid in full. Most people would not have been as diligent to save that same $10 or $20 at home and then come and pay for the item in full. It is the same with saving, the small amounts of money will build to bigger amounts over time once you *Transform you Money Mindset* and the process becomes a habit.

Go back to "saving for a rainy day". Saving for a rainy day is the same as emergency savings. Now many other financial experts will tell you that you should have 6 months of expenses saved in case something happens. For example, if you have $3,500 in expenses each month, that would be $21,000 in savings. They are not wrong to tell you that but for most people that number is so huge that your mind says "that's impossible" and so what do you save…nothing!

Remember:
Smaller amounts = consistent savings.

What I encourage everyone to do is to think about your housing payment (rent or mortgage). Your housing payment is usually your largest monthly expense. I encourage everyone to set a financial goal to have one month's housing payment in their savings. If your housing payment is $1,500 that should be your goal for emergency savings. Breaking the savings goal into smaller amounts makes it more achievable. When you think of $1,500 your mind says "I can do that".

If you are living with family and do not have to pay full rent or mortgage, think about what you rent or mortgage payment would be if you were on your own and save that amount.

As you read Chapter 5 and identify your financial goals, consider including a savings goal of one month's housing payment. *Hint*: Once you get your first month's housing payment saved, start saving for a second month!

Money Mindset Transformation Exercise Chapter 2: Your Savings Plan. Commit to a regular savings plan.
(Allow at least 1 hour. You will need pen and paper. You will need to think outside of the box.)

1. Decide how much you will save each pay period. For example, saving $25 per pay period. If you are paid every two weeks (26 paychecks) that will be $650 at the end of the year. If you are paid every week (52 paychecks) that will be $1,300 at the end of the year. If you are paid twice a month (24 paychecks) that will be $600 at the end of the year. Saving $25 a pay period adds up!
2. Have that amount automatically deducted from your paycheck and deposited into your savings account.

3. Download the **25 *Ways to Save*** form from our website www.fiercelyfinancial.com/resources. Look at your expenses and spending and think of *25 Ways to Save* right now. Without any additional income. You may have to do a little research on some things but I guarantee you will come up with *25 Ways to Save* in places that you did not imagine.

   Once you come up with your *25 Ways to Save* – total the amount you are saving each month just from your list and write down your total savings.
4. We would love to hear the creative ways you found to save. Send me an email at coaching@fiercelyfinancial.com or post on our Facebook Page – Fiercely Financial Coaching your *25 Ways to Save*!

   Hint: Often companies will give you savings but they will not offer it to you, you have to ask! For example, I had my cable service for many years and I would get offers in the mail addressed to occupant for specials at a better rate than I was paying. Finally, last year I called the cable company and asked if I could get the special rate. They told me this special rate was for new customers but they reviewed my account and gave me a reduced rate.

Chapter Three
Forgiveness

Think about where you are financially. Are you where you want to be? If you are not where you want to be financially, do you know why? Do you have a lot of credit card debt and you do not remember what you charged? Did you co-sign a car loan for a relative or friend and they stopped making the payments and the car was repossessed and that is now on your credit? Did you lose a home to foreclosure because you lost your job? Did you loan a relative or friend your rent money and they promised to pay it back but did not and you were evicted from your apartment? Did you cash out retirement accounts too soon?

Did you have to take out a loan to bury a loved and other family members promised to help pay back the loan and now the loan is delinquent? Were you injured in a car accident and could not work for 3 months and now you are in collections with many of your accounts?

These are real life scenarios and you may see yourself in one, two or more of these situations or you know someone who is in one or more of these situations. This is what we mean when we say "life happens". Sometimes these life situations are beyond our control and sometimes they are situations that we play a part in. Either way these situations do not make you feel good. When you look at what you did and/or what someone else did many feelings of anger, bitterness, hurt, guilt and failure can surround us. If you trusted someone who turned out to be untrustworthy you feel these emotions.

If you were left to handle a situation because someone we trusted did not handle their business (in the case of not having life insurance) you feel these emotions. If you went against your better judgment or someone's advice and moved forward in a situation that turned out badly for you financially, then you feel these emotions.

Feeling these emotions when your finances are not where you want them to be are normal. However, getting dragged down by these emotions will hinder you from moving forward and making the changes that you desire.

When you operate from a place of negativity, that negative energy surrounds you. It is similar to putting a high fence around your home and when the delivery driver comes to deliver your package they cannot give it to you because there is no way for them to get to your door. That is how negative energy works. While you might say you want to improve your financial situation, you cannot because your negative energy is stopping any positive action that you might be taking.

Your next step to *Transform Your Money Mindset* is to FORGIVE. The first person you have to forgive is yourself. Everyone makes mistakes. Yes, there are consequences to our mistakes but mistakes are a part of being human. Many times we do the wrong thing for the right reason. It is hard to deny someone you love and trust when they ask for your help. Do not beat yourself up because you tried to help. Helping is a good thing but you must learn to be wiser and learn from those situations.

My Dad always asked us in negative situations "what did you learn from that?" This was so we could think about how we could think and act differently for a better outcome the next time.

Learn your lessons but forgive yourself for making choices that worked against you financially.

Next you must forgive the other persons involved in these financial missteps. Many of these persons probably had good intentions. They intended to keep their promise to pay back the money or make the loan payment. Life gets in the way and when things spiral out of control for someone, they can barely keep the promises they make to themselves let alone to you. Even good people make mistakes and make promises they do not keep. Forgive them all today.

You will probably not release all of these emotions that you have immediately after reading this. It is a process. For every negative thought that you have when you get that feeling of anger or failure or guilt, just replace it with a positive thought. When you feel like "I can't believe I made such a mess of my finances", replace that with "I am taking action each day towards my financial fitness". Remember positive change cannot happen until you release the negative energy.

Money Mindset Transformation Exercise Chapter 3: <u>Write your Forgiveness Letters</u>.
(Allow at least 1 hour. You will need pen and paper. You will need to go deep within yourself. Choose a time when you won't be interrupted and you don't need to go anywhere after.)

1. Breathe deeply.
2. Make a list of your financial missteps.
3. Write a letter of forgiveness to yourself for the financial missteps you have made. At the end of the letter to yourself, include "I am a good person and I forgive myself and I am committed to being financially fit."
4. Read your letter out loud.
5. Breathe deeply.
6. Write a letter of forgiveness to anyone else that may have been involved in your financial missteps. If there is more than one person, you can write a separate letter to each person or one letter for everyone. At the end of the letter include "I forgive you."
7. Read the letter(s) out loud.

8. Breathe deeply.
9. You may not feel better immediately but you will over time.

Chapter Four
Thoughts + Beliefs + Actions
("The Triple")

Every year in horse racing there is chatter about a potential "Triple Crown" winner. That discussion is about the one horse that could potentially win all of the three biggest races – Kentucky Derby, Preakness and Belmont Stakes. During basketball season it is always newsworthy when a player has a "triple double" night. Meaning they have earned double figures in points, assists and rebounds. When you think about your money and finances you want to think about the triple as it relates to your Money Mindset. The Money Mindset Triple is Thoughts + Beliefs + Actions. If you want to *Transform your Money Mindset* your Thoughts + Beliefs + Actions must be aligned.

You might not be sure if you are aligned or not so here is an example. Thought - "I really want to be debt free." Belief - "I have so much debt, I will never be able to pay it off." Action - You continue to use your credit cards. Based on this your Money Mindset is not aligned. While your Thought is to be debt free, neither your Belief nor your Action support your Thought and so you will continue to be in debt.

When you are aligned this is what will happen. Thought - "I really want to be debt free." Belief - "I will be debt free in 5 years". Action - You stop charging on your credit cards and create a plan to reduce your debt in 5 years. Then your

Money Mindset is aligned and you will move toward your goal of being debt free.

The alignment of your Thoughts + Beliefs + Actions is the key because you must have all three working together to *Transform your Money Mindset* and move yourself forward in changing your financial situation. If you just Think it, it will not work. If you Think and Believe but you put no Action toward making it happen, it still will not work.

The old saying "something is better than nothing or two is better than one" does not work in this case. You have to have all three aligned! They have to work in harmony. Think of a choir, even it one person is singing off key, you can hear it. As well, when there is perfect harmony of voices and instruments you are mesmerized by their artistry.

What you are seeking with your Money Mindset is the perfect harmony of your Thoughts + Beliefs + Actions which will lead you to the financial change that you desire. Once you gain clarity on how each supports the other you will begin to see a shift in your financial situation. Start with your Thoughts and get clear about what you want. Then focus on your Beliefs being mindful to create Beliefs that support your Thoughts.

If your Beliefs limit or hinder your Thoughts, change that to a supporting Belief. Lastly, decide what Actions you must take for your Thoughts and Beliefs to become your reality for your finances. You must be committed to taking the Actions to realize the change you are seeking in your finances. You get results from what you complete.

Remember:
Thoughts + Beliefs + Actions that are aligned = RESULTS

Money Mindset Transformation Exercise Chapter 4:   Your Thoughts + Beliefs + Actions.
(Allow at least 1 hour. You will need pen and paper. You will need to go deep within.)

1. Download the **Thoughts + Beliefs + Actions** Worksheet our website www.fiercelyfinancial.com/resources.
2. Write down the Thoughts you have about the change you seek in your money and finances.
3. Write down the corresponding Beliefs about those Thoughts.
4. You will work on Actions in Chapter Five.

Chapter Five
Your Dreams
(Financial Goals)

What Financial Goals do you have?

- Purchase your first home?
- Save for your children's college education?
- Payoff your debt?
- Increase your emergency savings?
- Put more money into your retirement?
- What about starting your own business?
- Taking care of your parents or grandparents?
- Pay cash for your next car?
- Buy new furniture for your home?
- Take your dream vacation?
- Serve others in a bigger way?

We all have goals and we should not feel bad because we want things. We should not put our dreams in categories like "good" or "bad"; meaning if you want to save for your children's college education that is good but if you want to take a dream vacation that is bad. We all have dreams and desires and there is nothing wrong with that. For most of us, we do not have an unlimited supply of money so we have to make a plan. Without a plan we will not accomplish most of the financial goals that we desire.

So how do you get started? First, you want to define or identify your financial goals. Financial goals are anything that you want to buy (a car) or do (take a vacation) that you do not have the money for. You have to develop a plan to get the money.

Think about what you want to accomplish (Thought). Then create your Belief to support your Thought. Once you have your Thought + Belief you need the Action. The Action is what steps you will take so that you can achieve your goals/dreams. Write out your goal, the total amount you need, when you want to accomplish it and how much it will cost you each month to save towards your goal.

There are two foundations that should be part of every strategy to achieve your financial goals – a spending plan (budget) and saving. Let's start first with your spending plan. Create a spending plan or budget for your household. Start this by tracking your spending for 30 days and reviewing your bank statements for the last 3 months. Tracking your spending will help to identify the items that you are paying cash for. Reviewing your bank statements for the last 3 months will give you the overall picture of the majority of your bills and expenses. Your spending plan lists all of your income and expenses. You can write it out on a form or create a spreadsheet on the computer.

This step is important because to accomplish your financial goals you may not have the option to increase your income so you want to set up your financial goals and the process for accomplishing them with the money that you have available to you now.

As well, the goal is for you to commit and make the sacrifices necessary to achieve your financial goals and dreams. If you get additional monies you can decide to put that in your savings account or put it toward your financial goal to get you there faster.

Once you have all of your income and expenses outlined there are 3 steps in your review of your expenses. Step 1 - Identify your "non-negotiables". Non-negotiables will most likely be the things that must be paid – rent, mortgage, utilities, car payments, credit cards but they can also be things that we do not need but we have made a financial commitment to like helping your parents or giving to a charitable cause. *Hint* – If all your expenses are non-negotiables, go back and read Chapter 4!

Step 2 – Consider the expenses you can eliminate. Step 3 – Think about the expenses you can reduce. Even with your non-negotiables still look at ways to reduce those costs, especially with expenses like utilities or car insurance. Once you have reviewed everything, stop and sleep on it. Then review it once more the next day to see if there is anything you missed.

When you identify the amount of money you have available for your financial goal each month, you can now determine how long it will take you to accomplish your goal. Once you have that now you need a strategy for saving. How will you save the money? If you are not clear about how you will save the money then you will find that over time you will put the money in and take it out with the "promise" to replace it. *Hint* – That almost never happens! Or you will skip a month with the "promise" to double up next month. We know that most likely this will NOT happen.

Choose a savings method where the money goes in automatically and you do not have easy access to it. As we mentioned in the Chapter 2 Money Mindset Transformation Exercise, consider a local bank that is not close to you. You are more likely to keep money there if you do not have easy access to it. If your goal is a dream vacation consider working with a reputable travel agent to see if they can set you up on a payment plan. If you want to save for a down payment for a home, think about the local bank that is far away and NO debit card for the account.

As you identify your financial goals think about why these goals are important to you. Often we set goals but we do not have clarity about why we want them. Writing down why this is important to you adds another level of energy to keeping you committed to your financial goals.

Knowing your "Why?" will keep you in Action. It will keep you steadfast when you get weary. It will keep your eye on the prize when you understand and know in your heart why these financial goals are important to you.

As you define/identify your financial goals, note that financial goals are often put into three categories based on the time it will take you to accomplish them:

Short Term (Less than 1 year)
Intermediate (1 year to 5 years)
Long Term (5+ years)

Here are two examples of creating your financial goals.
Example #1 – Short-term:
Increasing emergency savings:

Financial Goals Worksheet				
Short-Term Goals (Less than 1 year)				
Goal/Strategies/ Why it is important to me?	**Total Cost**	**Duration (# months)**	**Monthly Cost**	**Target Date**
Increase Emergency Savings Strategies: ▪ Create a budget. ▪ Set up automatic payroll deduction.	$1,000	10 months (Feb – Nov)	$100	Nov 2016

Why it is important to me: <ul><li>I will have monies available in case of an emergency.</li><li>I won't have to not pay a bill to pay for the unexpected expense.</li><li>Peace of mind.</li></ul>				

Example #2 – Intermediate:
Save for down payment for home:

Financial Goals Worksheet				
Intermediate Goals (1 year to 5 years)				
Goal/Strategies/ Why it is important to me?	**Total Cost**	**Duration (# months)**	**Monthly Cost**	**Target Date**
Save for down payment for home Strategies:<ul><li>Create a budget.</li><li>Set up automatic payroll deduction.</li></ul>Why it is important to	$15,000	3 years (36 months)	$417	June 2019

me: • A better environment for my children. • A long-term investment. • Leaving a legacy for my children. • Showing my children what is possible.				

As you can see many of the strategies will be the same, just a longer time period and a higher amount of money monthly.

Remember that if you have a spouse or children, there has to be buy-in on the new spending plan from everyone and this may be a little challenging. As the parent you make the financial decisions but changes that will impact your children still need to be addressed. Remember Chapter 1 "Your Childhood Money Story" this now becomes your children's money story. Did they all of sudden have no cable television or could not go to an art class and all Mommy or Daddy said was "because I said so". Yes, sometimes sacrifices have to be made for the greater good but think about your 8 year old self or your 15 year old self and what would have been helpful to you to still feel loved and understood.

If your goal is taking a vacation or buying a home have your children look at brochures of the vacation destination or have them draw a picture of the house and put the pictures up around the home. When they ask for something that has been eliminated, you can say "Remember we are going to Disney World in July". That keeps their focus on the abundance of going on vacation not the lack of not being able to go to the movies.

This book was written primarily for you to digest as an individual. However, if you are part of a couple, then any transformation and change that you go through will impact the other person. My suggestion is that the other person read the book too or maybe you select passages of the book to discuss so that you both can share your thoughts.

It is important for couples to have regular "money talks" about finances. The first step is to think and act like a team. Even if each of you brought debt into the relationship, you are a team now and you have to think like a team. Or if one of you is earning more than the other or currently unemployed you are *equal* members of the team.

These "money talks" should not be to point the finger or assign blame but to establish an open dialogue about something that is an integral part of your lives and relationship. Even if you have tried in the past and it has not worked, try again to continue the discussion. It may be helpful to set some ground rules first and establish a "stop" word.

A "stop" word is used when someone is feeling uncomfortable and you establish before the conversation starts that if someone says the "stop" word then you stop that conversation for the moment. For example, when we have family gatherings and we feel like someone might be getting upset by a particular topic or that we have talked about something too long then everyone knows that our "stop" word is the weather. In those moments, someone will say "the weather sure is nice today" and everyone knows to change the subject. It does work.

It is important to note that often financial discussions will make you uncomfortable but try to push past your discomfort so that you can move forward. It is only when we push past our comfort zone that change happens. If we only do what is comfortable we become stuck and it makes it difficult to take the action needed to achieve our goals.

A good way to start the "money talk" might be to have each person share what financial goals and dreams they have and why they are important to them. Starting the discussion this way helps to keep the conversation positive. Then discuss the strategies of how to make your goals and dreams a reality.

*Caution: Just because you are in Money Mindset Transformation mode does not mean the other person is. You might have to go slow with bringing them on board.

Or it may be better to just let them witness your financial transformation.

Remember:
Peace and harmony
should always be a priority.

Money Mindset Transformation Exercise Chapter 5:   Your Financial Goals and Spending Plan.
(Allow at least 1 hour. You will need pen and paper.)

1. Download the **Financial Goals Worksheet** and the **Spending Plan** spreadsheet from our website www.fiercelyfinancial.com/resources.
2. Using your Thoughts from Chapter Four, write down the financial goals that you want to accomplish on the Financial Goals Worksheets.
3. Write down your strategies to accomplish your financial goals.
4. Write down why you want to accomplish these financial goals.

Chapter Six
Reasons

When we are trying to achieve financial goals and strengthen our financial position we often find that we are in "start and stop" mode. We start off good for awhile and somewhere along the way we get off track. When that happens we become discouraged, frustrated and just stop trying altogether.

For example, you set a financial goal of saving $100 each month beginning in January. You save $100 in January then another $100 in February and then another $100 in March. That is $300 and you are feeling good right? Then April comes and something comes up and you don't save the $100 and you say "I'll save $200 in May to make up for it".

When May comes, something else comes up and you do not save anything and you end of taking $100 out of your savings. You say "I'll catch up in June." When June comes you don't put in anything and take out $100. When July comes you throw up your hands and use the last $100. That's the "start and stop" mode.

When you consistently operate in "start and stop" mode you never accomplish your goals. Most often when you are in "start and stop" mode you have "Reasons" for why you did not move forward or stay consistent. If you are honest about your "Reasons" that seem valid, you will see that they are really excuses. When you constantly give "Reasons" for why you did not stick to your financial goals then you will find it challenging to accomplish your goals and achieve the financial fitness you are seeking.

Here are some common "Reasons" we use for not staying consistent with the strategies we outlined for our financial goals:

- "I work hard and I deserve to treat myself."
- "I was never taught how to manage money."
- "I have never been a good saver."
- "My parents weren't good with money and neither am I."
- "If I got paid more money, I would do better."
- "I'm going to pay off my credit card balance in full anyway."
- "I want to give my children more than I had."
- "You only live once."
- "I am too busy to deal with my finances."
- "I've tried spending less, but I just can't."

Remember:
"Reasons" are keeping you from being
Financially Fit.

"Reasons" are keeping you from your
Financial Greatness.

"Reasons" *Do not* bring results.

Every day is a new day and you can start again. You can decide today to let go of all your "Reasons" and Transform your Money Mindset. You do not have to wait until January 1st to get started with anything that you want to do. Start right now. If it is July and you decide to wait until January 1st that is 6 months of valuable time that you can never get back. If it is July 10th do not wait until August 1st. Make today your start date. Do not wait. You can do it.

It is important to acknowledge there are times when circumstances beyond your control will make sticking to your financial goals impossible. Unfortunate events like the death of your spouse, the loss of your job, a major illness. These are real situations that can impact you financially, mentally, emotionally and physically. It is in these times that you have to shift your focus to the crisis at hand and put all of your attention on working through this situation.

In these cases, getting off track is understandable and it may take some time for you to get back on track. During this time you should not worry about anything but yourself and your loved ones. When you are ready and able, you can get back on track with your financial situation and hopefully the good work that you started will be helpful in your time of need.

Money Mindset Transformation Exercise Chapter 6:   Your "Reasons".
(Allow at least 1 hour. You will need pen and paper.)

1. Download the **"Reasons"** Worksheet from our website:
   www.fiercelyfinancial.com/resources.
2. Circle all of the "Reasons" you have used in the past. (Add any additional ones.)
3. Write down what you will do the next time a "Reason" comes up that is causing you to detour from your financial goal.

Chapter Seven
"Where is the Money?"

Often I sit with clients and many will say they cannot save or pay off their debt or do not understand where all of their money goes. We review their spending they are always amazed at what they see.

The biggest eye opener is usually how much money they spend on food outside of the home. Food is tricky because food is a necessity. It is not like going out and shopping for high priced electronics or jewelry. We have to eat right? Yes we do but eating out 5 to 7 days a week is different than going to the grocery store, buying food and cooking your food at home.

For example, if it costs you $25 to eat dinner at a restaurant 5 days a week, that's $125 a week or $500 every 4 weeks. But if you decide to cut that to 2 days a week, that's $50 a week or $200 every 4 weeks. That is a savings of $300. I think about this a lot when I buy a salad out. When I buy a salad where you can select your toppings, I can pay about $8 to $10 for a salad. If I buy one head of lettuce that is about $1.69 and I can have at least 3 servings from that. You see the difference?

The other thing about food that throws us off is sometimes we spend in small amounts so we do not realize how those small amounts add up. If you get a coffee and a bagel for breakfast from the food cart each work day, that's 5 days each week. Typically a coffee and a bagel costs $2.00 so each week that is $10. Not too bad. Then you buy your lunch. Lunch every day costs $5.00 a day or $25 a week. That is $35 a week or $140 every 4 weeks for breakfast and lunch. In a year breakfast and lunch cost you $1,820. Remember if you are spending more for breakfast and lunch then your total cost is even higher.

We do not think about the breakfast or lunch because in the big picture $2 or $5 is not a lot of money. But as you can see, these amounts add up over time. So, think about how you can reduce your outside food bill. You do not have to eliminate everything. You can think of ways to reduce.

Some people like the bagels they sell in the bags in the bread section. As someone from the east coast, those are not authentic bagels! If you like those then buy a bag and a tub of cream cheese and now you have your breakfast for the week for more than half the cost. You can also buy your bagels from a good bagel maker for probably about 60 cents.

You can still buy your coffee/tea because that is easier to handle especially if you are getting to work on public transportation. If you drive to work, consider making your coffee/tea at home. When I was working in an office, I purchased an electric teapot and brought my tea, sugar and cup with me.

Another surprise for my clients is the number of times they go to the ATM machine and withdraw amounts under $100. $20 here, $40 here, $60 here. If you withdraw $40 twice a week that is $80 a week and $320 every 4 weeks, which is $4,160 a year.

When you take out cash, you do not always know where that money went. I encourage my clients to do both - track their spending for 30 days and review their last 3 months bank statements. Tracking your spending for 30 days will help you to account for where you are spending your cash.

What about technology? I have seen a lot of new technology and I love it. Sometimes I do not know what I would do without it. If my email is down I feel like the world has stopped. You get so used to it but some of the new technology has caused us to spin more out of control with our finances.

First, there were ATM machines. The convenience of ATM machines has given us easy access to our money. Who remembers the days when there were no ATM machines? I do! When Friday came, my parents would have to go to the bank and withdraw the money they needed for the weekend. And if there was a Monday Holiday the banks would be closed an extra day so my parents really had to plan their money. Because of this, we did more budgeting and planning with our spending.

Second, debit cards. Was there a time before those debit cards? Yes, and that was the time we wrote checks. We carried our checkbooks with us and recorded each check in our checkbook register. Also, duplicate checks came much later. When I taught financial education for workforce development students, many of the younger students had never seen a personal check or a checkbook register.

When debit cards came out, we were told that as soon as you swipe your debit card the monies immediately come out of your bank account. We have found that is not always true and because we are no longer walking around with our checkbook registers, we are not recording the amount each time we swipe our debit cards. This has lead to overdraft charges.

We can use our debit card anywhere! At the gas station, the supermarket, at all retail stores, restaurants, the movies, online, by phone – anywhere! I love the convenience that technology has brought to our banking system. However, the easy access to our money and easy access to make purchases has caused us to lose some of the controls that were in place to make us more fiscally responsible. Now we must rely on our own self-control and for some of us that is difficult.

Before you go to the ATM machine or swipe your debit card at the register or make an online purchase, stop and take 5 deep breaths and see if you still want to take money out the bank or make that purchase. Sometimes a 10 second pause can move you closer towards Transforming your Money Mindset and financial fitness.

Money Mindset Transformation Exercise Chapter 7:   Your Checkbook Register.

1. Go back to the box that your checks came in and pull out your check register. (Yes it's in there!)
2. If you cannot find it go to your bank and ask for one.
3. Keep your checkbook register with you and every time you swipe your debit card, pay a bill by phone or online or make an online purchase or write a check, stop and write it in your checkbook register. No matter where you are write down every transaction.
4. If you take out cash, record what it is used for.
5. If you have automatic debits coming from your bank account, keep a list of what they are for, the amounts and the dates of the debit from your account.

Chapter 8
Who are your People?

When we use the term "my People", most often it means our family members, friends and people from our community.   In this context this questions means who are the people in your circle who will support you as you seek to *Transform Your Money Mindset* and achieve financial fitness. Think about this. When you have tried in the past to set and achieve your financial goals (or any goals really), who in your circle supported your efforts? And more importantly, who in your circle either did not support your efforts or were accepting of your lack of commitment?

Here is an example.   Your financial goal – Payoff credit card debt in 2 years.   Your strategies – Stop using credit cards; create a spending plan to put $150 more towards credit card debt monthly; no shopping for clothes, shoes, jewelry, accessories for 6 months. See how each of "Your People" respond:

Your Blockers:
Friend/Family: "I need some new clothes. Let's go shopping."
You: "I told you I don't want to go shopping because I made a goal so I can payoff my credit card debt in 2 years and one of my strategies is not to go clothes shopping for 6 months.
Friend/Family: "6 months??? That's forever.

You: "It's not that long but I really have to try to stick with my plan this time."

Friend/Family: You know you always find something cute and I always get better deals when you are with me. Do it for me please!"

You: "Ok but I can't buy anything. Well, maybe something for $30."

Your Co-signors:

You: I got an email that my favorite store has an extra 40% off on sale items. I really want to go but you know I'm supposed to be on my financial plan which means no shopping for 6 months."

Friend/Family: "Buying a few things won't matter especially since the sale is now and things won't be on sale in 6 months."

You: "That's right. I'm actually saving myself money by buying on sale."

Your Supporters:

You: "I haven't been shopping in 2 months. This is hard."

Friend/Family: "Keep your eye on the prize. You have been doing good so far and you know you have a plan to be debt-free. You have been doing great so far and you can do it. Once you start seeing your debt going down even more, you will realize that the sacrifice of no shopping is worth it."

You: "Yes you are right I need to stay focused and stick to my commitment. Thanks for keeping me on track."

You see the difference? *Your People* should be the ones who will keep you accountable and on track. The one you can call when you are about to do something that will take you away from your goal and they can help you to refocus. These are the people who you need in your circle. You have to figure out how to turn the *Co-Signors* and *Blockers* into *Your Supporters*.

This can be delicate and sensitive and you probably will not be able to convert everyone and some of the ones you cannot convert you may still have to interact with them. So, when you are tempted and you do not have your Supporters around, stop and take 5 deep breaths, think about the reward you are working towards and most times this will be enough to get you back on track.

Money Mindset Transformation Exercise Chapter 8: <u>Your People</u>.
(Allow at least 1 hour. You will need pen and paper. You will need to go deep within.)

1. Download the **My People Worksheet** from our website: www.fiercelyfinancial.com/resources.
2. Look at the three categories. Think about your family and friends that you spend the most time with.
3. Put them in one of the 3 categories.
4. Your Supporters – Thank them for supporting you. Share your financial goals worksheet with them and ask

them to continue to support you in achieving your financial goals.

5. Your Co-Signors – Tell them you appreciate that they care about your happiness. Share your financial goals worksheet with them. Tell them that your financial goals and dreams are very important to you. Ask them to help you stay on track with your financial goals.

6. Your Blockers – You need to think carefully and honestly about your Blockers. Are these people who love you and have your best interest at heart? Or are they people who secretly do not want you to succeed because they fear where that will leave them? If you share with them your financial goals and dreams will they understand? Can they ever be Supporters?

Only you can answer these questions. If you have to be around your Blockers, then you should have your Supporters on speed dial to keep you accountable.

Chapter 9
You are the CEO of your Finances!

Many of us have worked jobs in retail or at fast food restaurants. When you work in retail or at a fast food restaurant, you know you have to be precise with your transactions and the money in your register. At the start of your shift before you can ring any purchases, you have to count all of the money in drawer so that you know how much you started with. Then you have to be sure to ring up each item at the right price. If there was a sale or discount, you have to be sure you entered that information correctly. You have to make sure you gave back the correct amount of change.

At the end of your shift, you have to count all of the money in your drawer again. You have to balance your drawer. You have to make sure that whatever amount the register tape shows you had in sales that you have that amount in your drawer in cash, checks or credit card receipts less any returns plus the original amount of money you started with. So, if you started your drawer with $200 and your register tape showed sales of $700 and returns of $100, then your drawer should have $800 in cash, checks and credit card receipts.

If you balance your drawer and you have $750 or $850 you know there is a problem and you have to figure out where the error is. Sometimes on your first week, management might let those mistakes slide because you are learning but if it happens after you have been there for a month it is highly likely that you would no longer have a job there.

Think about how careful you were with your drawer and ringing up. You were careful because you knew that your job required you to be careful. You knew you had to handle the company's money right! The company requires that and you want to keep your job.

Now think about the CEO of the retail or fast food company you are work for. A good CEO knows what is going on financially with their company all of the time. Each day the company CEO gets briefed and has meetings about the company finances.

The CEO watches their stock and their sales. They hear what the customers are saying about their products and service. They know which departments are doing well and the ones that are not. They know which stores are doing well and the ones that are not. And when they meet with their team, they want to know what is working well and what's not.

The company CEO knows there is a problem right away because she is on top of the finances of the company. Remember, she is getting this information daily. When the company CEO realizes the company is having a problem financially the first thing the CEO does is take action. She does not sit in her office with the "Do Not Disturb" sign on the door or watch television or go to sleep. No, she gets busy handling the situation head on. She starts to review everything.

First she reviews the internal things - their people, their products, and their service. Then she reviews the external things – the economy, location, customer likes and dislikes. And she does this all with her team. See, the CEO knows that she is good at what she does but she also knows that she is not an expert at everything so she surrounds herself with a strong team.

The CEO also reviews the company expenses with her team. What needs to stay as is? What needs to be eliminated? What needs to be reduced? Once the CEO has all of the information she needs, she develops a strategic plan to handle the situation. And she checks back on things more often to see if the plan is working.

You are the CEO of your Finances. In that role, you want to know everything that is going on. What is your income? Do you have a spending plan that outlines all of your expenses for the month? Does your spending plan include regular savings? Do you know the due dates of your bills? Do you know the due dates and the amounts of the automatic debits from your bank account? Do you review your bank statements weekly or at least monthly to be sure there are no issues? Do you balance your actual expenses with your planned expenses according to your spending plan?

What adjustments are needed to your spending plan? What adjustments are needed to your daily spending? Are there expenses that you can eliminate or reduce? Do you have a list of your credit cards and loans that includes the interest rate, current balance and monthly payment? Where are your tax returns and W2s for the last three (3) years? Do you know what withholdings you have on your paycheck? Are your payroll withholdings too low (always get a huge tax refund) or too high (always owe taxes).

Maybe you have not been in charge of your finances like the CEO but you can start today. Take action. Remember what the company CEO did when there was a problem – she took action! That is what CEOs do. They do not sit back, they take action. The company CEO knows she does not have all of the answers so she has a Team.

We all need help. Sometimes we might feel ashamed or embarrassed so we do not ask for help. Think about the company CEO who makes millions of dollars and manages millions of dollars. She is not ashamed or embarrassed to call on her team because she understands that to do her job correctly she has to call on the people who have the answers she needs.

That is what you have to do too. Asking for help makes you a person of action. It is only in action that you will move forward. Maybe it is overwhelming for you. That is ok. You do not have to do everything today. Take 1 action step as CEO of your finances today. Tomorrow, take another action step. The next day, take another action step. Each day, take action. You are the CEO of Your Finances!

Money Mindset Transformation Exercise Chapter 9: You are the CEO.
(Allow at least 1 hour. You will need pen and paper. You will need to go deep within.)

1. Go to our website: www.fiercelyfinancial.com/resources and download the sign **"I am the CEO of MY Finances"** and put that on your wall. Every day look at that sign and read it out loud three (3) times.
2. Schedule your financial fitness strategy time. What is your financial fitness strategy time? The time you schedule (yes schedule) on your calendar at least once a month to review your finances and your financial goals.
3. Put your financial fitness strategy time on your calendar every month for the rest of the year. Allow at least 1 hour and schedule it for the same day/time each month i.e. the first Saturday at 9am.
4. When someone asks you to do something during that time, "you say that's my financial fitness strategy time and I have to be there". They will want to know what you mean so share with

them. It may encourage them to do the same!

5. If you find that you need help or have questions – ask!

Chapter 10
Share your Knowledge!

When we see a good movie, we tell someone. When we eat at a restaurant and the food and service are excellent, we tell someone. When we find a great hair salon, we tell someone. When we read a good book, we tell someone. When we buy a great computer, we tell someone. We share so much information but we will not talk about money and finance. Why?

Money and finances has in our families and in our communities fallen into the "mind your business category" or the "don't tell your business" category. Why is that? With money and finance being such an integral part of our lives when did it become taboo to talk about it? When did it become a secret? When did it become something that we felt we could not share or ask about?

I do not know why it is like this or when it happened but I do know that there have been consequences because we have kept the discussion about money and finance off limits. And many of these consequences are carried down through generations.

What I think could be a possible cause is that many people feel that discussions about money and finance will lead to questions about how much money you make or how much money you have. People feel questions about our salaries and how much money we have is private information so we do not want to open any door of conversation where we might be asked about that.

Consider this. If you have adopted a more healthy lifestyle you would talk about what you are doing differently like eating more fruits and vegetables, drinking more water and exercising more regularly. You do not have to say how much you weigh or what size clothes you wear and the majority of the people you are talking to would not ask you.

That is how we need to think about money. When we talk about the ways that we manage our money and finances we do not have to disclose how much we earn or how much we have. If someone asks, we can just say nicely "oh that's not important" or just change the subject. We have to get past it so that we can grow, learn and educate others.

Teaching our children about money and finance is very important. Parents sometimes ask when they should start talking to their children about money. When a child is old enough to start asking for things, especially when they go to a store which is usually age 3 or 4, that's the time to start. For kids (and adults!) you have to make it fun, short and age appropriate. Be consistent. There are always opportunities to teach.

Before you go to the store with your child, you can give them $2 and tell them this is your money to spend on whatever you want. When you are in the store and your child sees something he wants and it costs $3, then talk to them. You can say, you only have $2 and that costs $3 and so you need another $1. Of course they will ask you if you have another $1 and you tell them they have to buy the item with their own money. You tell them, they can put the $3 item back and get a $2 item or they can wait to buy the $3 item when they get another $1.

As well, not every time you take your child to the store should they buy something. Think about yourself. If every time you go into a store, you buy something you want, that is not going to support your financially fit lifestyle. This is a teaching time for your child. Have the discussion before you go to the store and let them know that they are not buying anything today.

I know parents want to give to their children but it does not help them with their Money Mindset if you give to them every time they ask. These are the same decisions they will have to make as they get older but then it will be $20 versus $30 or $100 versus $150.

Start your children with a mind of saving early. Relatives and friends are constantly giving children money for birthdays, for holidays and just because. Discuss with your children that a portion of all money received must be saved. You can decide how much. If you get them started early saving 50% of the monies they receive, this will become a habit for them.

Tell family and friends that you are teaching your child to save 50% of the money they receive. Ask family and friends that when they give your child money that they break up the denominations so that it is easy for the child to know what they can keep and what they can save.

For example, if they give your child $10 have them give them two $5 bills so it is easy for your child to understand saving 50%. Additionally, the person giving the gift can also say to your child "remember you have to save half". This repetition helps your child to understand the savings principle and that it is a requirement.

Having your child save their money in a piggy bank is good for them until they start school. Once they start kindergarten or 1st or 2nd grade, take your child to the bank and have them open a savings account. When they receive gift money, take them to the bank and help them make the deposit. This gets them to understand that the money they are saving should go into a savings account at the bank.

Be sure your bank sends a bank statement and review the bank statement with your child. Review each deposit, show them how their account balance increased with each deposit and discuss how interest adds more money.

Seeing the money in their savings account grow will encourage your child to continue.

There are many computer-based financial education programs for children. And there is always Monopoly. This can serve as both a financial education and a family time activity. There are many versions of Monopoly and you can choose the one that is best for your child. You can also find out from your child's school what they are offering for financial education.

Many schools have included that as part of the curriculum but not all. But schools may be willing if the parents ask. When I was in 2nd grade, we opened savings accounts at school and we brought our money to deposit to school. I kept that bank account until I was in high school. You might suggest visiting a bank as a field trip for the students.

We have to think of easy non-intrusive ways to share information about money and finances with our family, friends and in our communities.

Here are some ideas on how to share money and financial information with your family, friends and in your community:

Email – Share the monthly emails from Fiercely Financial Coaching with your friends and family. (If you are not on our email list, sign up at coaching@fiercelyfinancial.com and we will add you today!)

Facebook – Like our page Fiercely Financial Coaching and share the Monday Money Mindset Tips and other educational information with your Facebook friends.

Instagram – Follow us at Fiercely Financial Coaching and share the educational information with your family and friends.

Twitter – Follow us @FiercelyFinance and share the educational information with your family and friends.

Book Clubs – If you are in a book club, select a book on a financial topic. It should be a short book that is an easy read. You might even be able to email the author and say "our book club has selected your book for our next discussion, would you be able to give me 10 questions that can help to shape our discussion". Most authors would be happy to provide that. I will!

Email me at coaching@fiercelyfinancial.com and ask for your book club discussion questions. If you are not in a book club you could have a one time book discussion on a financial education book, like this one!

Family Reunions – Ask a professional to come in and do a brief presentation on a financial topic. I have done this for my family reunions and I have presented on credit, credit score, homeownership and foreclosure. If you cannot get a professional to come in or you do not have a lot of time on your agenda, then download some of the information in our free resources section from our website www.fiercelyfinancial.com/resources , copy them and distribute them.

Hair Salon/Barber Shop – Ask your stylist or barber if you can put out some literature on financial topics in the salon/shop. Again you can download our free resources from our website:
www.fiercelyfinancial.com/resources or share resources that you receive from another professional and leave them at the salon/shop. Great topics are credit and credit score, renter's insurance, budgeting, savings, reducing debt and paying for college.

Game Night – Monopoly is a great game to engage children and adults. You can also coordinate this for faith-based and community events. It teaches financial education and it is a great family activity.

Seminars/Workshops – Attend a seminar or workshop on a financial education topic with a family member or friend. There are many quality free or low-cost options. Check out our website at www.fiercelyfinancial.com or on Facebook at Fiercely Financial Coaching for dates on where we are presenting in your area. As well, your local library or community college may have financial education events.

_____

Money Mindset Transformation Exercise
Chapter 10: Share your Knowledge.
(This is an ongoing exercise.)

1. Commit to one thing you can do each month to share money and financial information with your family and friends.
2. Share what you are doing on our Facebook Page (Fiercely Financial Coaching).
3. Post what you are doing to **Share your Knowledge** on our Facebook page (Fiercely Financial Coaching).

Conclusion

Now that you have read *"Transform Your Money Mindset"* it is my desire that the book will give you hope about all that is possible. Hope that you can achieve the financial goals and dreams that you desire. Hope that you do not have to feel ashamed or guilty because you have made mistakes that have negatively impacted your finances.

Hope that it is never too late. You can start now doing things differently and get back on track. Remember that positive and lasting change is never easy or fast. Steady and consistent progress will lead you to the changes that you are seeking and the financial success that you desire.

As you move forward, keeping yourself motivated and encouraged will be critical to your success. Consider the reasons your financial goals and dreams are important to you. What are your "whys"? Your reasons are just as important as the goals and dreams. For most of you your "whys" will be for your children, your family, your community and maybe even the world. Write down your "whys" and place them on your wall or put pictures of your "whys" on the wall. This will keep you focused on your goals and dreams.

I encourage you to get an accountability partner. Think of someone who is on their own journey for better financial fitness. Check in daily or twice weekly for 15 or 30 minutes to discuss your actions and your progress. Having someone to support you and hold you accountable will help you stay on track and keep focused. If you feel like you are getting off track, you should check in with your accountability partner for support. Or consider coordinating a Money Club where 5 to 10 of you meet weekly by phone and once monthly in person to discuss your progress and support each other.

As you embark on your journey to better financial fitness, remember to celebrate the small accomplishments and milestones. Write them down and put them up on the wall where you can see them. Share your success with a family member or friend.

Finally, share your knowledge! Think about the ways that you can share with others how they can transform their Money Mindset and share with them important financial education information. Share with your children, your family, your friends and your community. Use the old principle – "Each one, teach one."

I would love to keep in touch with you. Visit our website at www.fiercelyfinancial.com and sign up to be a part of our email list to receive our monthly e-newsletter and periodic financial education information.

If you are interested in having me speak at your next conference or forum, please email us at coaching@fiercelyfinancial.com.

If you are interested in our financial coaching programs, email us at: coaching@fiercelyfinancial.com to schedule a Get Acquainted Call.

If you are interested in our financial wellness programming for your employees, email us at coaching@fiercelyfinancial.com to learn more about our onsite financial education programs.

Like us on Facebook at Fiercely Financial Coaching.

Follow us on Twitter @FiercelyFinance.

Follow us on Instagram at Fiercely Financial Coaching.

I welcome your feedback on the book and more importantly please share your Money Mindset progress.

Email me at coaching@fiercelyfinancial.com or post on our Facebook page – Fiercely Financial Coaching.